All I Know About Women

After years of dating and a marriage I've finally realized I know NOTHING about women!!!!!!!

All I Know About Women

After years of dating and a marriage I've finally realized I
know NOTHING about women!!!!!!!

All I Know About Women

After years of dating and a marriage I've finally realized I know NOTHING about women!!!!!!!

All I Know About Women

After years of dating and a marriage I've finally realized I
know NOTHING about women!!!!!!!

All I Know About Women

After years of dating and a marriage I've finally realized I know NOTHING about women!!!!!!!

All I Know About Women

After years of dating and a marriage I've finally realized I know NOTHING about women!!!!!!!

All I Know About Women

After years of dating and a marriage I've finally realized I know NOTHING about women!!!!!!!

All I Know About Women

After years of dating and a marriage I've finally realized I know NOTHING about women!!!!!!!

All I Know About Women

After years of dating and a marriage I've finally realized I
know NOTHING about women!!!!!!!

All I Know About Women

After years of dating and a marriage I've finally realized I know NOTHING about women!!!!!!!

All I Know About Women

After years of dating and a marriage I've finally realized I
know NOTHING about women!!!!!!!

All I Know About Women

After years of dating and a marriage I've finally realized I know NOTHING about women!!!!!!!

All I Know About Women

After years of dating and a marriage I've finally realized I
know NOTHING about women!!!!!!!

All I Know About Women

After years of dating and a marriage I've finally realized I know NOTHING about women!!!!!!!

All I Know About Women

After years of dating and a marriage I've finally realized I
know NOTHING about women!!!!!!!

All I Know About Women

After years of dating and a marriage I've finally realized I know NOTHING about women!!!!!!!

All I Know About Women

After years of dating and a marriage I've finally realized I know NOTHING about women!!!!!!!

All I Know About Women

After years of dating and a marriage I've finally realized I know NOTHING about women!!!!!!!

All I Know About Women

After years of dating and a marriage I've finally realized I know NOTHING about women!!!!!!!

All I Know About Women

After years of dating and a marriage I've finally realized I
know NOTHING about women!!!!!!!

All I Know About Women

After years of dating and a marriage I've finally realized I know NOTHING about women!!!!!!!

All I Know About Women

After years of dating and a marriage I've finally realized I know NOTHING about women!!!!!!!

All I Know About Women

After years of dating and a marriage I've finally realized I
know NOTHING about women!!!!!!!

All I Know About Women

After years of dating and a marriage I've finally realized I know NOTHING about women!!!!!!!

All I Know About Women

After years of dating and a marriage I've finally realized I know NOTHING about women!!!!!!!

All I Know About Women

After years of dating and a marriage I've finally realized I know NOTHING about women!!!!!!!

All I Know About Women

After years of dating and a marriage I've finally realized I know NOTHING about women!!!!!!!

All I Know About Women

After years of dating and a marriage I've finally realized I know NOTHING about women!!!!!!!

All I Know About Women

After years of dating and a marriage I've finally realized I
know NOTHING about women!!!!!!!

All I Know About Women

After years of dating and a marriage I've finally realized I know NOTHING about women!!!!!!!

All I Know About Women

After years of dating and a marriage I've finally realized I
know NOTHING about women!!!!!!!

All I Know About Women

After years of dating and a marriage I've finally realized I know NOTHING about women!!!!!!!

All I Know About Women

After years of dating and a marriage I've finally realized I
know NOTHING about women!!!!!!!

All I Know About Women

After years of dating and a marriage I've finally realized I know NOTHING about women!!!!!!!

All I Know About Women

After years of dating and a marriage I've finally realized I know NOTHING about women!!!!!!!

All I Know About Women

After years of dating and a marriage I've finally realized I
know NOTHING about women!!!!!!!

All I Know About Women

After years of dating and a marriage I've finally realized I
know NOTHING about women!!!!!!!

All I Know About Women

After years of dating and a marriage I've finally realized I know NOTHING about women!!!!!!!

All I Know About Women

After years of dating and a marriage I've finally realized I know NOTHING about women!!!!!!!

All I Know About Women

After years of dating and a marriage I've finally realized I know NOTHING about women!!!!!!!

.

All I Know About Women

After years of dating and a marriage I've finally realized I know NOTHING about women!!!!!!!

All I Know About Women

After years of dating and a marriage I've finally realized I know NOTHING about women!!!!!!!

All I Know About Women

After years of dating and a marriage I've finally realized I
know NOTHING about women!!!!!!!

All I Know About Women

After years of dating and a marriage I've finally realized I
know NOTHING about women!!!!!!!

All I Know About Women

After years of dating and a marriage I've finally realized I know NOTHING about women!!!!!!!

All I Know About Women

After years of dating and a marriage I've finally realized I know NOTHING about women!!!!!!!

All I Know About Women

After years of dating and a marriage I've finally realized I know NOTHING about women!!!!!!!

All I Know About Women

After years of dating and a marriage I've finally realized I know NOTHING about women!!!!!!!

All I Know About Women

After years of dating and a marriage I've finally realized I
know NOTHING about women!!!!!!!

All I Know About Women

After years of dating and a marriage I've finally realized I know NOTHING about women!!!!!!!

All I Know About Women

After years of dating and a marriage I've finally realized I
know NOTHING about women!!!!!!!

All I Know About Women

After years of dating and a marriage I've finally realized I know NOTHING about women!!!!!!!

All I Know About Women

After years of dating and a marriage I've finally realized I know NOTHING about women!!!!!!!

All I Know About Women

After years of dating and a marriage I've finally realized I know NOTHING about women!!!!!!!

All I Know About Women

After years of dating and a marriage I've finally realized I know NOTHING about women!!!!!!!

All I Know About Women

After years of dating and a marriage I've finally realized I know NOTHING about women!!!!!!!

All I Know About Women

After years of dating and a marriage I've finally realized I know NOTHING about women!!!!!!!

All I Know About Women

After years of dating and a marriage I've finally realized I know NOTHING about women!!!!!!!

All I Know About Women

After years of dating and a marriage I've finally realized I
know NOTHING about women!!!!!!!

All I Know About Women

After years of dating and a marriage I've finally realized I know NOTHING about women!!!!!!!

All I Know About Women

After years of dating and a marriage I've finally realized I know NOTHING about women!!!!!!!

All I Know About Women

After years of dating and a marriage I've finally realized I
know NOTHING about women!!!!!!!

All I Know About Women

After years of dating and a marriage I've finally realized I know NOTHING about women!!!!!!!

All I Know About Women

After years of dating and a marriage I've finally realized I know NOTHING about women!!!!!!!

All I Know About Women

After years of dating and a marriage I've finally realized I
know NOTHING about women!!!!!!!

All I Know About Women

After years of dating and a marriage I've finally realized I know NOTHING about women!!!!!!!

All I Know About Women

After years of dating and a marriage I've finally realized I
know NOTHING about women!!!!!!!

All I Know About Women

After years of dating and a marriage I've finally realized I know NOTHING about women!!!!!!!

All I Know About Women

After years of dating and a marriage I've finally realized I
know NOTHING about women!!!!!!!

All I Know About Women

After years of dating and a marriage I've finally realized I know NOTHING about women!!!!!!!

All I Know About Women

After years of dating and a marriage I've finally realized I
know NOTHING about women!!!!!!!

All I Know About Women

After years of dating and a marriage I've finally realized I know NOTHING about women!!!!!!!

All I Know About Women

After years of dating and a marriage I've finally realized I
know NOTHING about women!!!!!!!

All I Know About Women

After years of dating and a marriage I've finally realized I know NOTHING about women!!!!!!!

All I Know About Women

After years of dating and a marriage I've finally realized I
know NOTHING about women!!!!!!!

All I Know About Women

After years of dating and a marriage I've finally realized I know NOTHING about women!!!!!!!

All I Know About Women

After years of dating and a marriage I've finally realized I know NOTHING about women!!!!!!!

All I Know About Women

After years of dating and a marriage I've finally realized I know NOTHING about women!!!!!!!

All I Know About Women

After years of dating and a marriage I've finally realized I
know NOTHING about women!!!!!!!

All I Know About Women

After years of dating and a marriage I've finally realized I know NOTHING about women!!!!!!!

All I Know About Women

After years of dating and a marriage I've finally realized I
know NOTHING about women!!!!!!!

All I Know About Women

After years of dating and a marriage I've finally realized I
know NOTHING about women!!!!!!!

All I Know About Women

After years of dating and a marriage I've finally realized I
know NOTHING about women!!!!!!!

All I Know About Women

After years of dating and a marriage I've finally realized I
know NOTHING about women!!!!!!!

All I Know About Women

After years of dating and a marriage I've finally realized I
know NOTHING about women!!!!!!!

All I Know About Women

After years of dating and a marriage I've finally realized I know NOTHING about women!!!!!!!

All I Know About Women

After years of dating and a marriage I've finally realized I know NOTHING about women!!!!!!!

All I Know About Women

After years of dating and a marriage I've finally realized I know NOTHING about women!!!!!!!

All I Know About Women

After years of dating and a marriage I've finally realized I
know NOTHING about women!!!!!!!

All I Know About Women

After years of dating and a marriage I've finally realized I know NOTHING about women!!!!!!!

All I Know About Women

After years of dating and a marriage I've finally realized I know NOTHING about women!!!!!!!

All I Know About Women

After years of dating and a marriage I've finally realized I know NOTHING about women!!!!!!!

All I Know About Women

After years of dating and a marriage I've finally realized I know NOTHING about women!!!!!!!

All I Know About Women

After years of dating and a marriage I've finally realized I
know NOTHING about women!!!!!!!

All I Know About Women

After years of dating and a marriage I've finally realized I know NOTHING about women!!!!!!!

All I Know About Women

After years of dating and a marriage I've finally realized I
know NOTHING about women!!!!!!!

All I Know About Women

After years of dating and a marriage I've finally realized I
know NOTHING about women!!!!!!!

All I Know About Women

After years of dating and a marriage I've finally realized I know NOTHING about women!!!!!!!

All I Know About Women

After years of dating and a marriage I've finally realized I
know NOTHING about women!!!!!!!

All I Know About Women

After years of dating and a marriage I've finally realized I know NOTHING about women!!!!!!!

All I Know About Women

After years of dating and a marriage I've finally realized I know NOTHING about women!!!!!!!

All I Know About Women

After years of dating and a marriage I've finally realized I know NOTHING about women!!!!!!!

All I Know About Women

After years of dating and a marriage I've finally realized I
know NOTHING about women!!!!!!!

All I Know About Women

After years of dating and a marriage I've finally realized I know NOTHING about women!!!!!!!

All I Know About Women

After years of dating and a marriage I've finally realized I know NOTHING about women!!!!!!!

All I Know About Women

After years of dating and a marriage I've finally realized I know NOTHING about women!!!!!!!

All I Know About Women

After years of dating and a marriage I've finally realized I
know NOTHING about women!!!!!!!

All I Know About Women

After years of dating and a marriage I've finally realized I know NOTHING about women!!!!!!!

All I Know About Women

After years of dating and a marriage I've finally realized I know NOTHING about women!!!!!!!

All I Know About Women

After years of dating and a marriage I've finally realized I know NOTHING about women!!!!!!!

All I Know About Women

After years of dating and a marriage I've finally realized I know NOTHING about women!!!!!!!

All I Know About Women

After years of dating and a marriage I've finally realized I
know NOTHING about women!!!!!!!

All I Know About Women

After years of dating and a marriage I've finally realized I
know NOTHING about women!!!!!!!

All I Know About Women

After years of dating and a marriage I've finally realized I know NOTHING about women!!!!!!!

All I Know About Women

After years of dating and a marriage I've finally realized I
know NOTHING about women!!!!!!!

All I Know About Women

After years of dating and a marriage I've finally realized I know NOTHING about women!!!!!!!

All I Know About Women

After years of dating and a marriage I've finally realized I know NOTHING about women!!!!!!!

All I Know About Women

After years of dating and a marriage I've finally realized I know NOTHING about women!!!!!!!

All I Know About Women

After years of dating and a marriage I've finally realized I know NOTHING about women!!!!!!!

All I Know About Women

After years of dating and a marriage I've finally realized I know NOTHING about women!!!!!!!

All I Know About Women

After years of dating and a marriage I've finally realized I
know NOTHING about women!!!!!!!

All I Know About Women

After years of dating and a marriage I've finally realized I know NOTHING about women!!!!!!!

All I Know About Women

After years of dating and a marriage I've finally realized I know NOTHING about women!!!!!!!

All I Know About Women

After years of dating and a marriage I've finally realized I know NOTHING about women!!!!!!!

All I Know About Women

After years of dating and a marriage I've finally realized I know NOTHING about women!!!!!!!

All I Know About Women

After years of dating and a marriage I've finally realized I know NOTHING about women!!!!!!!

All I Know About Women

After years of dating and a marriage I've finally realized I know NOTHING about women!!!!!!!

All I Know About Women

After years of dating and a marriage I've finally realized I know NOTHING about women!!!!!!!

All I Know About Women

After years of dating and a marriage I've finally realized I
know NOTHING about women!!!!!!!

All I Know About Women

After years of dating and a marriage I've finally realized I know NOTHING about women!!!!!!!

All I Know About Women

After years of dating and a marriage I've finally realized I know NOTHING about women!!!!!!!

All I Know About Women

After years of dating and a marriage I've finally realized I
know NOTHING about women!!!!!!!

All I Know About Women

After years of dating and a marriage I've finally realized I know NOTHING about women!!!!!!!

All I Know About Women

After years of dating and a marriage I've finally realized I
know NOTHING about women!!!!!!!

All I Know About Women

After years of dating and a marriage I've finally realized I know NOTHING about women!!!!!!!

All I Know About Women

After years of dating and a marriage I've finally realized I know NOTHING about women!!!!!!!

All I Know About Women

After years of dating and a marriage I've finally realized I
know NOTHING about women!!!!!!!

All I Know About Women

After years of dating and a marriage I've finally realized I know NOTHING about women!!!!!!!

All I Know About Women

After years of dating and a marriage I've finally realized I
know NOTHING about women!!!!!!!

All I Know About Women

After years of dating and a marriage I've finally realized I know NOTHING about women!!!!!!!